Sweet Island Life

The History Of
**Cat Island
Bahamas**

NEVELON T. GAITOR

ISBN: 978-0-9847460-9-5

Design and Layout by Michael J. Matulka of Basik Studios (*www.gobasik.com*)
Omaha, Nebraska USA

Published by Nevelon T. Gaitor
Nassau, Bahamas

Printed in the USA

10 9 8 7 6 5 4 3 2 1

Acknowledgments

Thanks to Almighty God for the wisdom, knowledge and the ability to produce, in written form, the cultural aspects of a rich and diverse heritage from which Bahamians can appreciate.

To my devoted wife Olive Carmetta Gaitor, to whom this book is dedicated, you have been the wind beneath my wings and I would forever cherish your warm and jubilant spirit. Thank you kindly for the tremendous support that allowed me the opportunity to accomplish my goals.

Sincere thanks and appreciation to Rev. Neil Hamilton, Justice of the Peace, for his continuous encouragement. Natives of Cat Island who have freely provided information on Bush Medicine. Wikipedia Image for a Map of Cat Island that captured its' significant beauty. To Dr. Charmaine Bodie for the willingness to assist with editing the accuracy of Bush Medicine terminology. Thank you to Ms. Bennique I. Brown, former Teacher of the Year, at the S. C. McPherson Jr. High School for her dedication and consistency throughout the editing process. May God's continued blessings rest on you.

Special thanks to Ms. Avis Lightbourn, Education Officer at the Department of Education.

Contents

Preface

Island life is so sweet. Growing up on the island is like a child's first glimpse of the stars at midnight. The Bahamas in the early sixties, seventies and eighties was a village bursting with excitement. You can tell by listening to the old folks reminiscing about the good old days. We went crabing in the bush, climbing the coconut tree, picked sapodilla and coco plumbs from the wild and made pepper sauce from the garden in the back yard.

Yet we forget, the mouth-watering sea grapes and berries from the wild. Eating freshly baked potato bread with light brown spicy stew fish was a delight, especially on a Sunday morning. Learning the art of swimming in the pond and jumping from the rocky edge of ocean holes brought the family together with joy.

Living on the island was not a bed of roses for some families. There were tough times because the mail boat did not come to the island for more than two weeks sometimes. The island had no electricity nor water supply in settlements along the coast line. Life was simply primitive, but the ability to persevere as a people strengthen the spirit of hope.

The Bush Medicine kept the family healthy. You could not resist the smell of bush tea early in the mornings just before day break. Pain and discomfort at the end of the day depended primarily on your choice of bush medicine.

Going to school and learning the golden rules cannot be overlooked because it was our passport to a greater and successful future. Mama would say, "Come here boy! You think you bad. Wait until your Papa come, he will beat you bad".

Each settlement on the island, people came together for a common goal. Attending church three times on a Sunday was the way of life for the old and young. People of the religious faith joined their voices with hymns of praise that echoed from the valley to the rugged hills of Viage Green, the original name for the settlement of Dumfries. Anglicans, Baptists and Church of God parishioners celebrated joyously at festivals. Some of the most exciting and memorable experiences of my childhood life are connected in part to the stories you will read about. I hope you enjoy my vatae of life on Cat Island.

The History of Cat Island

With less than 2,000 local inhabitants and only 70 miles of island stretched across the Caribbean, Cat Island is quaint and known for its natural and historical landmarks including Mt. Alvernia, the highest point in the Bahamas. It is also visited for its remarkable architecture, created by famous architect Monsignor Jerome Hawkes, an Anglican priest. It may not be one of the more popular Caribbean destinations for tourists, but Cat Island's history may very well be the most fascinating of any of the Bahamian Island.

IN THE BEGINNING

Like other islands scattered throughout the Bahamas, Cat Island is believed to have been inhabited as early as the 9th Century AD by tribes referred to by many names including the "Arawaks", "Lucayans", and the self-imposed "Lukku-Cariri". The island still features some of the ancient structures believed to have served as primitive shelters for these peaceful indigenous people. In fact, much of the history of Cat Island can be told through the large untouched, ancient and colonial remnants of the past.

DISCOVERY AND SETTLEMENT

It is believed by many that Cat Island, not San Salvador, was Christopher Columbus first place of landing when he discovered the New World, thus, "Columbus Point" is located on the southern part of the island. There is debate about how the island's current name originated, and the most popular theory is that it was named after pirate Arthur Catt who came to the island to bury his treasures. While it is feasible that the island's name was derived from its cat-like shape, as seen from the air, others believe that the island was once overrun with wild cats.

Although the Spanish first explored the island, they never settled there, and the whole of the Bahamas became a British Crown Colony after religious refugees landed there in 1717. During the American Revolution, Loyalists from Virginia also came to the island and attempted to establish cotton plantations. Because the plantations were not successful, their agricultural aspirations eventually led them to sow fields of peas, corn, and potatoes which were tended by freed slaves after their emancipation in 1834. These early farmers would send their harvest to Nassau to be sold at the marketplace. Agriculture is still a major part of Cat Island's economy today and is maintained through slash-burn farming.

ARCHITECTURE

Famous architect and hermit Monsignor James Hawks, also known as Father Jerome, made a significant contribution to the history of Cat Island. He is largely responsible for the beautiful architecture that remains on the island to this day. Among many other designs, Father Jerome built The Hermitage in 1939 on top of Mt. Alvernia, a 206 ft. mountain, recognized as the highest point in the Bahamas. There, he lived and meditated, and became known as "the conscience of the island" due to his ongoing willingness to help resolve conflicts and assist those in need.

LEGACY

Many of the modern-day tourist who visit Cat Island do so because of its architectural significance and its well-preserved historical landscape. The island also boasts of being the birth place of celebrity actor Sir Sidney Poitier whose father once lived in a settlement on Cat Island known as Arthur's Town. The famous musician called "Exuma the Obeah Man", whose real name is Tonny McKay, was born on the island in 1940. Many deem Cat Island to be the original source of all Bahamian music.

Today the popular Rake- An- Scrape music origin is from Cat Island. This popular music has resulted in what is dubbed "The Rake- An- Scrape Festival". Come with me and you will experience the preserved talents at its best.

Map of Cat Island

Bain Town
Orange Creek
ARTHURS TOWN
Zion Hill
Dumfries
Bennett's Harbour
Thurston Hill
Roker's Bluff
Industrious Hill
The Cove
Knowle's Village
Smith's Bay
Fernandez Bay
New Bight
Old Bight
Greenwood
Mc Queens
Houks Nest
Devil's Point
Port Howe
Bahntown
Cutless Bay

Sweet Island Life

CHAPTER 1
The Miracle at Birth

The sky was dark gray just before dawn. The sound of thunder shook the wooden table in the front room of the small limestone house at the end of the dusty road. Rain drops splattered the palm trees near the wooden window next to my father's bed. The sun was covered with a blanket of dark clouds and the wind could be heard whistling through the coconut trees next to the graveyard. Lightening flashed east, west, north and south; it struck the two headed coconut tree from top to bottom. It was without a doubt, the most unpredictable weather for the season. I would never forget it, the loud sounds of rumbling thunder that swelled my head and rattled my legs.

My father had just returned with the midwife to spend time with the family before the birth of the baby. There was not a moment to lose. The weather was extremely bad and he was not sure if the building next to the kitchen would stand the force of the wind. Everyone in the little house kneeled down as the midwife prayed for calm.

Mother was about to give birth within the hour. The midwife had unpacked her bag which contained bush medicine and the equipment that she had used repeatedly to assist with delivery of babies. I looked through a tiny opening in the wooden wall and saw what appeared to be my mother's face with tears running down her cheek. My father stood near the old iron bed with a hand full of cotton balls ready to assist the midwife.

Bam! Bam! Ba- am! The thunder rolled loudly and the lightening flashed intensely, lighting up the wooden room. I closed my eyes and fell asleep for a moment. There it was on the arch of a rainbow my little baby brother. I suddenly awoke from my amazing dream and heard the midwife scream and shout in a firm voice, "Caesar is his name".

I knew my mothers' belly had grown very large but did not anticipate it took eight months, three weeks, and six days of pregnancy. As I walked into the little wooden room and stood at my mothers' bedside, it became quite clear that mothers' belly looked like a deflated balloon. I did not know what had happened in such a short space of time. And so I asked the midwife who smiled and said, "You have a little baby brother."

As I exited the limestone house, the clouds floated slowly across the western skies and the cool breeze brushed against my face like feathers from a Peacock. All of the neighbors, mostly women, raised their hands in the air, shouted from the top of their voices and danced in front of the house I called home.

My mother was very proud to have an addition to the family. She placed Caesar on her breast and rubbed his tiny back. I quickly moved over to the iron bed eagerly anticipating mother's next move. The midwife looked at me, took the bundle of joy from my mother's arms, and removed the blue blanket that swirled around his tiny body.

I knew that I would be the first to look into my brother's eyes, hold his tender fingers and watch his lips open to inhale the fresh air in the room. As evening approached, I gazed at the small bowl of water and green leaves on the wooden table. My mind was fully engaged because I wanted to know what it was on the table, if it were mother's medicine.

The next day I went into the room and examined the bowl. To my surprise the water had turned light brown. Mother smiled and gave her approval for me to taste it. I did not hesitate for a moment but instead grabbed the bowl and drank until nothing was left.

Oh! Oh! To my amazement it was very bitter. Eventually, I started to cough and my eyes bulged out of its socket. I was suffering from a predicament that would not be repeated without knowing about the after effect. Mother later explained to me that the liquid was a mixture of "Cap nit" leaves steeped overnight in water. It was used by the Midwife on the island as a remedy for babies who would have experienced discomfort to the stomach.

There were no Gerber and Beach Nut brand of baby food or Similac milk back in the old days. Mother fed the baby with "flour Pap", a soft mixture of flour and water. Mother drank lime tea and ate a small portion of the flour bread for breakfast. My baby brother was fed about six spoonful of tea that had been made from a plant commonly called "Dill Seed" which was placed in boiling water.

I looked into my brother's tiny eyes and imagined him to be Caesar the great because that name was chosen from the Bible. His name was different because he had been given only one name, I had several names. Grandma, my parents, the midwife and the other siblings could not agree on the names I should have been given. Therefore, my father wrote all of the names in the family Bible and those names were sent to the recording office in Nassau to be placed on my birth certificate.

Caesar was strong, wise and friendly but at times he became lonely and desperate for attention. As he grew the family could tell that he would not be the ordinary boy who likes to participate in the activities in the home. Perhaps, what really excited Caesar the most, was the ability to predict the weather condition before it happened and his investigative skills to solve difficult mathematical problems at an early age.

Sweet Island Life

CHAPTER 2
School Life on the Island

Ting- a ling- a -ling. The school bell ring. I remember the Headmaster standing on the steps of the school building with a large hand bell. I was excited because it was the end of summer and the journey to the farm in the rain and scorching sun would not be as frequent.

We assembled in the school yard with our books and pencils ready to begin school on the first day. The all age school population was approximately forty students of different ages and ability levels. I was placed in grade five not because of age, but my ability to comprehend, predict, solve problems, and read fluently.

Every morning we gathered at the entrance of the one room schoolhouse where we would sing or repeat the multiplication tables. The Headmaster was a disciplinarian, teacher, farmer, preacher, and parent. He knew everyone in the settlements on the island and no one dared to misbehave or not attend school.

While seated on the wooden bench in my class awaiting story time, a frog jumped from the rafters above and landed on my forehead. I screamed loudly, and that got the attention of everyone in the building. It was uncommon to have been greeted with an unbelievable surprise on the morning when I was a few minutes late for school. The Headmaster had already given me the first verbal warning for my tardiness. I realized that even in the quiet moments in life, you can be faced with circumstances and situations that perhaps would be rather uncomfortable.

I can clearly remember classes under the coconut and sapodilla tree. One class was situated to the east and the other in the west under the umbrella of green leaves. Those moments were memorable, especially under the sapodilla tree where the fruit grow in bunches of two and three. The smell of a ripe sapodilla could distract your attention from a lesson when you are hungry. As usual the choice is yours. The juicy fruits on the tree vary in size and shape. I enjoyed dozens of the sapodilla "dilly" during the break and lunch time at school.

Let us not forget fun time. The older children formed a circle, then they held hands. I watched with amazement hoping that they would have asked me to join them. I felt excluded and wanted to know why they did not want me to play. My cousin approached me from behind and whispered, "It's ring play time." You would get your chance to play. At that point, my eyes expanded like an elastic band and I felt my heart beating rapidly against the muscles in my chest.

Suddenly I realized that the game had begun and voices were heard chanting the songs as they moved in a clockwise motion. Now it was my time to join them. They loudly sang, "Brown girl in the ring, Brown girl in the ring and she look like a sugar in a plum. Show me your motion…" Without delay I jumped into the center of ring, shaked my buttock, wiggled my body in front of the person who would be next.

The game of shooting marbles were no surprise at all. At school the boys took a delight in shooting marbles for fun. I remember my friends James and Matthew involvement in the game during lunch break. We stood watching them without realizing that the lunch break had ended. The Headmaster stood quietly next to where the boys were and shouted their names. At first, no one moved. I suddenly felt intense pain on my buttock and the rest was history.

Cleaning the school yard was no different from doing the same at home. We were taught that cleanliness is next to Godliness. The last Friday in each month at school, we were scheduled to clean the wooden benches and scrubbed the smooth concrete floor. It was fun for the entire school. I laughed and skated on the wet floor without the teachers noticing. School days are the best days of our life.

My Senior High School days were remarkable. The memories of meeting new friends and embracing the opportunities available to get an education was my first priority. There were few distractions other than walking the sandy beaches and watching the birds fly across the waters to the other side of the creek. You could not find a single television on the island. Therefore the local news was broadcast on a radio powered by four large size batteries.

At school, you came in contact with many characters. Some of them were pleasant while others were simply unpredictable. Remembering the good old days at school on the island, it made me come to the realization that life is but a vapor. In the morning, it covers the valley with thick mist but in the afternoon it disappears.

I looked into the eyes of my friend of the opposite sex with a passion of a thousand angels and saw sparkles like that of stars floating across a blue sky in mid-summer. She was the one that captured the rhythm of my heart. Immediately, I could feel my temperature rising. There was no need to call a fire engine because the affection for her was real. While others may have experienced the passion for romance, my primary goal was not to focus on the unknown but to bravely chart a course for the future.

Lunch time at school was awesome. We visited the petty shops in the settlement and purchased flour bread, coconut cake and a quarter pound of sausage. You can only imagine the pleasure we felt to have sausage, bread and a cold cup of water to drink. The reality was to ensure that we ate something before returning to classes for the remainder of the day.

My friends Patrick, Norman, Lloyd and Tyrone knew the struggle we had encountered at school but we were determined to overcome the challenges and make a difference. Let us not forget that success lies not in being the best, but in doing our best.

CHAPTER 3
Life in the Community

Sitting on the dock of the bay watching the tide as it rises and falls with the shadow of the evening sun. I could not have chosen a better place to retreat from difficult days on the farm. Growing up on Cat Island was not a mistake but a reality. Home of the "Rake And Scrape," incredible white sandy beaches and crystal clear waters, rolling hills, delicious flour cake, stew-fish and Jonny cake, bush tea, just to name a few; was the place that I knew as home. There is nothing in the city that can replace all the things that commonly made Cat Island different. Living there with the people that you love is unique, and I believe such a life style filled with rich heritage cannot be found anywhere else in the Caribbean or the world.

Growing up in a community located just east of Arthur's Town and west of Bennett's Harbor was the perfect environment for my humble beginning. The settlement of Dumfries is significant in my life story. The place I call down home is symbolic to me because it means that I participated fully in the activities on the farm, walked the dusty road with a bundle of wood on my head, swept the yard, collected water from the well, fished from the rocks on the sea coast, went for crab at nights with a torch, attended Sunday School, grinded corn to make grits and shot marbles in the school yard.

Down home was the place to be every day. Growing up there meant that attending regular church services was mandatory. I became excited when it was time to attend the annual convention of different religions in the settlement. The people in the community came together and gave their support. It was fun time when the Burial Society celebrated their festival. People in the settlement participated on the parade from the church to Burial Society Hall collected dozens of flour cakes, drank some booze and danced until it was dark. The young adults engaged in romantic conversations while the children played games and drank the tasty Bahamian made switcher.

Of course, I cannot forget the times when someone died and the "wake" had to be held the next day. The folks called the event "setting up". If you weren't there you would have missed a life time of the old fashioned songs that struck at the heart of a real Bahamian setting up.

Moments as these, captured the soul of your imagination. Papa sat near the door with his walking stick which was carved from a tree branch call fire wood. He always kept order in the meeting house during the regular Sunday Services.

At the " Wake", a wooden table would be placed in the center of the room and the natives would gathered to sing Negro spirituals. They were the people who decided which songs the congregation would sing at the setting up. I usually chose to sit on the wooden crate next to my cousin Ormando Brown. As I gazed at faces across the room, a firm voice at the table announced the song "When the Home Gate Swing Open for Me". Voices then joined in the harmony and soon the melody of this most popular song filled the air. I shall never forget how the community bonded together and celebrated the home going memorial of a loved one.

CHAPTER 4
Down Home Nightlife

We all knew how to dress for a night on the town in the city but it was different on the island. Nightlife on the island is indigenous to Rake and Scrape music and the "heal and toe polka" which is common on Cat Island. The locals here on the island believed that the Rake and Scrape music is the finest on the land. You can listen to the sound of the goat skin drum as the beat shuffled the rhythmic vibe so that the dancers can position each footstep for the next move.

The Grand Master of the Quadrille, Mel Gaitor, circle the dance floor and position himself in the center of the stage. Sam, Carlton, Tanya, Pearl and Aunt Lucy shuffled their feet to signal the number one dance move. Of course there were many more quadrille moves and only those who were skillful enough would be able to dance up to six.

Just then, I eased myself between the chair and the jukebox to watch with excitement because I was ready to capture all of the dance movements. Amazingly, this Cat Island prince, signaled to his partner to join him at the center of the dance floor. The motion of his slim body swirled as he danced to the rhythm of the goat skin drum, along with the intense scraping of the saw. The other dancers joined the competition that lasted for approximately twenty minutes. The music was so sweet that the audience did not realize the song competition had ended.

Later that night I visited aunt Rolle's Place near the Turning Point. The music at this distinguished night spot was hot, hot, hot! The live band had a jam session and the locals and visitors alike were having a great time. The legendary late great Tony "The Obeah Man" McKay was born just two blocks in a building near Aunt Roll's club.

That night I played cards with the locals and had a great time. The time was well spent as the people danced to the music of "Ancient Man" recording artist Kenyon McDonald. I had heard so many stories about the Cat Island "Rake-An- Scrape" and the rich culture of Bahamian music. Just as I was about to leave the popular night spot, surprisingly an elderly lady walked into the room and shouted, "I don't want no raking and scraping in here." Everyone became silent until she left the room. Moments later, the band played the song "I Don't Want No Rakin' n' Scrapin, in Here" and everyone danced, pranced, and wiggled their bodies to the rhythm which was their favorite of night.

I cannot forget the tasty flour cake, the delicious coconut and banana bread, the sheep tongue souse, the bush tea and a cup of the bush medicine called, "twenty one gun salute". The older folks have referred to it as the magic medicine because it gives men strength to the back.

At midnight everyone was tired, as sweat gathered on their brow and many of them wanted to go home to rest until another night. I knew that it was time to go home and rest but the excitement was awesome.

The next night was as exciting as the first. I attended a family function for a few hours before visiting another popular night spot on the island. I had a great time playing cards with the natives and listening to the amazing stories about the island.

I could not believe that it was after midnight and the weather condition was not the best for outdoor activity. My friend and I had decided to walk home rather than ride on the back of a truck in the rain. Just as we turned the corner that lead to the wooden house next to the graveyard, the dogs began to bark and the roasters crowed repeatedly for a few minutes. We were afraid because someone dressed in dark clothing had followed us from the popular night spot to the corner next to the grave yard only to discover that it was papa Jones who wanted to ensure that we arrived home safely. I shall never forget the experiences of night life on the island.

CHAPTER 5
The Magic of Bush Medicine

The magic of bush medicine cannot be forgotten by the people who have practiced the craft of providing a cure for many diseases and discomfort over decades. We must appreciate the tremendous stride as a people to be exposed to modern medicine of the twenty-first century. I believe that the history of bush medicine should be taught in our schools as a unit, and generations unborn will be inspired to commit themselves to further research with the hope that new discoveries are found.

I remember my parents searching the backyard and traveling miles to the north side to find the right kind of bush in order to produce bush medicine. But for God's grace and the wisdom given to the people, bush medicine saved lives. So, come with me and you would discover the names of some of the plants that the natives used to produce bush medicine.

BREADFRUIT LEAVES
The leaves are steeped in boiling water
and used as a beverage to reduce cases
of high blood pressure.

CATNIP
The plant is used to treat diabetes,
and tea for stomachache in babies.

BO' HOG BUSH
The plant is used to stimulate the loss of appetite.

ALOE (Vera)

The gel is used to apply directly to skinburn and it
alleviates pain and cure sores on the body.

POUND-CAKE BUSH

This plant is used to combat "weakness"
felt in the body and can be used as a remedy for
coughs. It is also used as wash for skin sores.

LIGNUM VITAE

The juice from the bark when boiled
is used as a laxative.

JUMBEY

The leaves are used as feed for cattle.
It can be used as a cure for "wind on the infant
stomach". Many natives used it for calming the
nerves and treating heart diseases.

PIGEON PLUM

The leaves when boiled is used
to stop "free bowels" in adults.

LIFE LEAF

It is used in "shortness of breath" and for
those individuals with kidney conditions.

SHEPHERD NEEDLE

This plant is used for prickly heat
'cooling the blood', to bring relief to 'sick stomach',
and as a relaxing drink every day for nine mornings
for worms in children.

GOAT PEPPER

The leaf on the plant is crushed
and placed on a boil to "draw" it to head.

HORSE BUSH

The plant leaves are used to bath
if there is cancer to the skin.

PERIWINKLE

This plant is used in the
treatment of leukemia.

GUINEP

The plant leaves are used when boiled in
hot water to reduce high blood pressure.

JACKMADA

It is used to increase the appetite and reduce fever.

GUINEA HEN BUSH

The root of the plant is crushed to a powder
and inhaled for the relief of headaches.

THISTLE

The orange-colored juicy substance is used as a cure
for ringworm; an infectious disease and jaundice.

WHITE SAGE

The leaves when boiled in hot water are used as a tea.
It can be used as a sponge bath in cases of measles
and chicken pox "itching of the skin".

DILL SEED

The small seeds can be used in brewing a
tea which has a smoothing effect on infants and the
natives used it as baby's "gripe water" when the child
experience discomfort to the stomach.

BAY RUM

It is used as a cooling skin bath.

BUTTER CUP

The leaves are boiled and used as a relief
for common cold, and for women when
experiencing monthly period pain.

STRONG BACK

The plant is used for individuals
who experiencing pain or "weakness"
in the back or waistline area.

MORNING GLORY

It is used for the relief of pain in a woman's
back due to "strain" or heavy lifting.

CERASEE

The plant is used extensively as a "tea".
Also it can be used as a cure for fever and cold.

LOVE VINE
It is used for an itch on the skin, as a cooling
bath and combined with other bush to make what
the natives call, "twenty-one gun salute".

SOAP BUSH
It is widely used for the common cold
and to wash the hair.

ROCK BUSH
It can be used as a mouthwash and
something to chew for stomachache.

STOPPER BUSH
It is used for "building up men's energy level"
and as a laxative for diarrhea in young children.

SNAKE ROOT
It is used as a tonic to cleanse
the body and reduce fever.

ROOSTER COMB
It is used on the skin in cases of
impetuous chicken pox.

OBEAH BUSH
The leaves are boiled in hot water
and it is used as a bath to cure pain in joint
or bones in the leg and hand.

FOWL FOOT
It is used to bathe women
immediately after childbirth.

PAPAYA
The juice is used as an aid to
digestion and a cure for ring worm.

GALE-WIND GRASS
It is used for poor appetite, constipation,
typhoid fever, flue and cold; It is a popular herbal
treatment because of it has no side effect.

FEVER GRASS
It is boiled in hot water and used as a tea for the flu.

CRAB BUSH
It is used for stomach pain.

FIVE FINGERS BUSH
It is used to make hot tea and to relieve backache.

NEEM
The leaves are manufactured to produce soap
and skin lotion. It is used to cure skin condition.

BAIGE A RENA
It is used for the flu and cold.

FRESH WATER FIG
It is used for pain in the stomach.

STIFF-COCK
The leaves are boiled and served
as a tea to purify the blood. The males
used it to increase erection of the penis

PUMPKIN SEED

The seed is crushed into a powder, it is boiled
to make tea. It help to build sperm count, prevent
prostate cancer and improve sex drive.

RAM HORN

The leaves are boiled and served as a tea.
It is used for stoppage in the urine of males

BRASILETTA BARK

It is used for tea at the family table. The wooden
bark is boiled. The tea is light pink in color.

PUMP GROUNDNUT

The fruit is boiled for tea and it is used
to fight against cancer to the liver.

PRICKLE BUSH

It is used to cure chickenpox and sores on the skin.

WHITE ELDER

It is used as a bath for chicken-pox
and consumed as a tea to reduce fever.

SLAVE BUSH

The shrub is used for coughs and
as a wash for sores on the skin.

WILD GUAVA

It is used to reduce high temperature
in the body as a result of a fever.

BAY ONION
It is used as a relief for lung congestion,
a cure for the common cold.

SOLDIER VINE
It is used to "restore manhood" if such is lacking.

OLD LADY MANGROVE
It is used to relieve severe backache in
women during pregnancy.

FOWL-FOOT
It is used as a bathe after pregnancy
and a tonic following childbirth.

SOURSOP
It is used as a relief of high blood pressure;
drink as a tonic at bed time.

PRICKLEY PEAR
It is used for sore joint and gout.

BUSH MEDICINE LEAVES & PLANTS

POND BUSH   PIGEON PLUM   LIGNUM VITAE

JUMBEY LEAVES
& FRUIT

BRASALETTA
BARK

LIME PLANT

SOURSOP

GRANNY BUSH

OLD LADY
MANGROVE

PRICKLY PEAR

FOWL-FOOT

JERUSALEM
MOON BUSH

PAPAYA FRUIT
& LEAF

OBEAH BUSH

CASCARILLA

27

APPETITE BUSH

STOPPER BUSH

BAY LILLEY BULB

SOLDIER VINE

LOVE VINE

STRONG BACK

BLACK
MANGROVE BUSH

GALE-OF-WIND

SMALL CANE

ROCK BUSH

SOAP BUSH

MORNING GLORY

SHEPHERD'S
NEEDLE

BUTTERCUP

NEME LEAVES

SPICE

SALVE BUSH

JACKMADA

BAY RUM

BLUE FLOWER

SNOWBERRY

WILD GUAVA

DILL SEED

GUINEA HEN

THISTLE

CERASEE ON
THE ROCK

WHITE ELDER
WITH BERRIES

HORSE BUSH

CATNIP

LIFE-LEAF

PERIWINKLE

ANGEL TRUMPET

RED PEPER

FIVE FINGERS

BREADFRUIT

MATCH ME BUSH

CHAPTER 6
Products of Nature

SAPODILLA TREE

TAMARIND TREE

THE CAT ISLAND
ROCK OVEN

BREADFRUIT TREE

Sweet Island Life

CHAPTER 7
Bahamian Folk Tale

In the good old days, "Story Time", was once a treasured cultural tradition in Bahamian communities. I believe that stories are of significant value because they promote community values, create a bond among the people, validate Bahamian culture and national identity.

Presently, many developmental changes have led to the disappearance of the wonderful oral stories. As a result, many of the younger generation have never heard a Bahamian Ole' Story and some do not even know that these stories have existed for decades.

It was a Friday morning, a beautiful day and a disastrous one for Caesar and Jake. Everyone in the settlement had heard about the story "Phantom of George Pond", and if they had not heard it, they would certainly believed it as the story unfolded.

George Pond was located four miles from the settlement on the northern side of the island. It was known as the watering ground for the animals, birds and the natives during the hot summer months. Children, were afraid to pass the watering hole because there were always strange noises that frightened them so much that they would cover their faces with the palm of their hands and hold on to their grandmothers' skirt.

Late one afternoon, Jake and Caesar had decided that they would remain on the farm near George Pond to catch crab and pick custard apple. Little did they know, that from after dark, George's spirit roamed the area until the break of dawn. Jake seemed to be afraid of the dark and he did not venture far away from Caesar's presence. He held his torch with a firm hand.

It was dark, strange noises were heard coming from beyond the hills. The air was filled with an unpleasant odor, the birds flew away in the darkness and the animals immediately ran into the bushes. Jake realized that the ghost of George Pond had arrived and no one would be able to stand in his way. Just then, the hair on Jake's head stood upright and his heart pounded against his chest like a goat skinned drum. It appeared as if the sky became a blanket of dark clouds, the moon turned into blood and the image of a man dressed in a robe of fire sat upright above a tomb stone in mid-air. It seems as though smoke poured out of his sharp pointed noise. Lightening flashed from the east and the sound of rapid thunder shook the ground beneath their feet.

Jake clearly remembered the stories told to them by their grandparents. He was speechless as he quickly recovered from the shocking experiences and assisted Caesar with the bag of crabs and with the dozens of custard apple that they had collected. Time was like an ever rolling stream that bears it's son away.

At the dawn of a new day, Caesar and Jake had realized that the events of the night would be the unforgettable experiences of their lives. There would never be a repeat of those frightening experiences again. The story of the Phantom of George Pond would live on for generations as it seeks to capture the imagination of a cultural significance and creates a bond among our people.

CHAPTER 8
Tradegy at Sea

The experiences of fishing from the edge on the rock is quite different from the knowledge gained on a fishing trip out on the ocean. Papa Joe can tell his story of both because he fished from the edge of the cliff along the coastline and was the captain of a native sloop called "The Raven".

Papa Joe and his son Natt frequently went on fishing trips to the southern side of the island near a small uninhabited cay. Early one morning they packed their bags and set sailed on a fishing trip which lasted for eight hours. This trip turned out to be a very special one for them because fish were plentiful on the fishing ground where they gathered every year to reproduce.

I wanted to experience a day in the life of a fisherman and this was my opportunity to venture out into the deep blue sea and catch the fish that I always dreamed about. The weather was fair as Papa Joe hoisted the sail of his sloop and skillfully guided the boat through the narrow channel to the open sea. Natt and I stood at the brow of the boat and watched the waves as the Raven increased speed towards the fishing ground.

We finally arrived at the fishing ground after two hours of sailing. I was very excited and wanted to impress Papa Joe. As a result, I accidently fell over board and had to be rescued from the chilly waters by Natt. Papa Joe was not concerned at all because he knew that I was an average swimmer and would eventually learn the skills needed on board the boat.

Now it was time to return home. We had caught enough fish to feed the entire settlement for two days. But just as I was about to pull my fishing line from the water, I hooked something huge. It was a large rock fish and it was difficult to pull it on board the boat. After a long struggle Papa Joe lifted my dream catch out of the water and smiled.

The sky was dark at the northern end of the island and the wind could be heard whistling in the air as the large canvas sail flapped against the wooden mask of the boat. I did not know that we would be caught in the midst of a storm. A short time later, it began to rain and I was frightened that something unexpected would happen. Papa Joe was confident that we would reach safe harbor but I could tell by the expression on his face.

Suddenly the boat hit an unknown object and the wooden mask snapped into two pieces and fell into the sea. Natt and I were thrown a few feet on the deck of the boat and Papa Joe was left hanging to the canvas in the water. Everyone needed a helping hand to survive the monster waves and chilly rain. The thunder rolled loudly and the lightening flashed intensely in the sky.

About ten minutes later, the boat over turned and Natt was swept away by the strong current. While on the other hand, Papa Joe and I held on to the wooden timber for safety. I feared that Natt would be lost forever in a watery grave in the deep blue sea. But hope kept us alive when it seemed as though, at any moment, we would be swallowed up by the giant waves.

A few hours later, Natt was discovered on a sandy beach a few miles from the entrance to the harbor with multiple broken ribs. He was Papa Joe's only child. I now realized that life is but a dream. Whether or not you fulfilled it, your dream is yours forever. Thus, it was a memorable experience that I shall never forget.

CHAPTER 9
Skeleton on the Back Seat of His Car

Folktales and stories of Anansi have become well known all-over the world, and often used in the schools by educators to teach moral concepts. We as a unique people can appreciate the experiences of our ancestors by the many encounters they had with the wonderful occurrences in nature.

Bahamian Folktales were created from the mysteriousness of people uniting for a service in songs called, "The Wake" after someone died. The service are usually held at night and ended a few hours before the funeral service in the morning.

Legend has it that any encounter with a ghost could cause your hair to raise on your head, the knees to buckled under the weight of your body and your eyes to budge out of its' sockets.

Mama Lucy had just died and Uncle Richard decided that he would attend the "Wake" that night in the settlement twenty miles from his home. He did not realize that he would travel alone because he was unable to convince his cousins to accompany him.

Richard eventually thought that it was best to travel to the "Wake" alone without anyone to disrupt him while he reflected on the memories of Mama Lucy whom he loved. Without a doubt, this was his quiet time to exhale and prepared himself for the role he would play at the funeral service.

There were no street lights erected on the long and winding road. Each settlement on the island had it's graveyard and most of them were located on the beach but a few could be found near to the roadway. As a matter of fact, the myth was that whenever someone approaches the grave yard, he would not point his fingers towards the tomb stone out of respect for the dead.

It was a dark and lonely night. Suddenly there were unusual sounds, like that of bones clashing, in a battle of the band. Those sounds caused Richards' hair to stand upright on his head. He glanced into the rear view mirror and there it was two skeletons sitting on the back seat of his car. A firm voice echoed "Let us out near the graveyard."

Richard must have fainted because to his amazement the car was found several hours later at the entrance to the grave yard. The story of Richards' encounter with skeletons on the back seat of his car became legendary.

CHAPTER 10
Cat Island Jack a Lantern

The Jack A Lantern story is the most famous mythological spirit of Cat Island; which captured the imagination of death and the afterlife. It has been stated that the spirit of the dead revisited the places known to him or her in life. Stories of such a mythological strength captures the attention of both young and the old. It is with a sense of pride to present stories which appealed to the audience and encourage them to listen as each scene is presented in stories or on stage.

The summer holidays were upon us and I was happy to be out of school in order to prepare my torch and packed the bags for the journey to the crabbing ground. I was excited because the weather was excellent for catching crab.

In the darkness, I lit the torch and hastened to a dusty road that lead to bushes in the mangrove swamp. To my amazement there were hundreds of crab in the area and I caught more crabs than I expected. Moments later, I had noticed a bright light about two hundred feet from where I stood. I then shouted loudly for the person to come and catch the crabs that were left in the area.

I was extremely worried after several bright lights appeared in bushes near the opposite side of the road from where I stood. At that point, I had noticed the lights were in the shape of a lantern as it moved slowly among the trees. The hair on my head stood upright and I was convinced that it was the ghost of Jack A Lantern.

Mama! Mama! I shouted, as tears rolled down my cheek like a stream from the rocky hills of Lucky Mount. I wanted to run away and hide but amazingly I was unable to take one step forward. My body became weak, therefore I slowly stretched my hands forward and embraced the trunk of a large lignum vitae tree.

Sweet Island Life

Later, I slowly opened my eyes and saw the reflection of the sun as the dark clouds floated across the sky which signaled the dawn of a new day. The dozens of crabs that I had caught disappeared leaving behind the empty bags. This was a horrifying experience that I could never forget.

CHAPTER 11
Escaped from the Grave

Uncle Ben had been told that he would live three score years and ten and by extension of good health, he may enjoy life beyond one hundred years. There have been many opinions about the secrets of life beyond expectation. However, no one knows the time nor the hour when life would expired.

It was a scream of passion, the ringing of the church bell and neighbors conversations that alerted the individuals in the settlement that Uncle Ben had died. People from the other settlements visited the family and expressed sympathy for his passing.

Everyone showed up for Uncle Ben's funeral service which was held at one of the local churches in the community. The tradition in those days was to ensure that the person who died must be buried the next day. There were no medical practitioner on the island to examine the body and actually issued a death certificate. Since this was the case in the southern islands in the Bahamas, Uncle Ben could have experienced a comma and did not actually died.

After several hours at the church, Uncle Bens' body was taken on a parade to the grave yard which was located half mile south of the main road. People lined the roadway to watch as the remains of Uncle Ben as it was taken to his final resting place. The expressions on the faces of neighbors and friends had revealed their pain and grief.

A body of water, called "The Pond" separated the settlement from the cemetery. The old concrete bridge served as the pathway to the sandy soil which was used by their ancestors for burial. Upon arrival at the cemetery, the old dark gray head stones stood upright with phrases like "Rest in Peace" and "Gone but not Forgotten". The symbols were there as a reminder that each person has a permanent resting place after death.

Uncle Bens' body was placed in a wood box built by the men who were members of an organization called "The Burial Society." The burial plot was prepared in advance by removing the sand to create a rectangular area six feet in depth and four feet wide. The wooden coffin was placed on two thick ropes and the men slowly placed it into the hole.

Everyone gathered around the grave as the spiritual leader committed the body to the ground; "Dust to dust, Ash to ash..." It was a sad occasion but also a frightening experience for those who attended the funeral.

As the men started to cover the coffin with sand, there were unusual noises which indicated that something strange was taking place. The wooden coffin at the bottom of the deep hole showed signs of movement and everyone at the grave yard were frightened because of the phenomenon. They watched with much anticipation. Uncle Ben was alive as he made his escape by forcing the top of the coffin open and sat upright with his hands raised above his head.

Bush cracked and man gone. Men, women and children dashed towards the entrance gate of the cemetery leaving behind the spiritual leader with Bible in his hand. Some of the women ran across the shallow pond leaving behind their shoes and hats floating in the water.

On the other hand, the spiritual leader seemed to have been hindered from leaving because his robe had become entangled on a tomb stone nearby. As frightened as he was, never did he leave behind anything that was precious to him.

Like the Resurrection story, the message went out that Uncle Ben was alive. While there were much excitement, neighbors and friends had gathered at Uncle Bens' house to anticipate the significant story of a life time. He was calm and never spoke about his unfortunate experiences to any stranger other than family members.

Just then Pokey said, "Well mother sick, you mean to tell me that Uncle Ben would have a second funeral service if he dies to night?" We were all amazed that he lived one year after this shocking experience. Upon the second announcement of Uncle Ben's death, the people made certain that there was not a second Resurrection for Uncle Ben.

Sweet Island Life

CHAPTER 12
Grandpa's Sermon

Grandpa's sermon was the most popular and exciting of all times that I could remember while living on the island. He was considered a Historian, Farmer, Policeman, Pastor, Choirmaster and a prominent individual in his community.

There were nightly services held during the annual district convention at grandpa's church. Each night a preacher was chosen to deliver the sermon to the congregation that filled the church. Some of the biblical text were stories like; "The Lost Sheep", Prodigal Son," "The Woman at the Well" and "The Resurrection of Jesus." Grandpa was chosen to speak on the final night of the convention and his text had been based on the story "Jonah and the Whale." He had delivered the most enthusiastic and persuasive sermon of his life time.

The Church was filled with persons from different parishes who had travelled several miles on the island to participate in the service and give moral support. Grandpa had almost completed his fiery and soul searching sermon when he repeatedly said, "Jonah swallowed Whale." The audience quickly corrected him and laughter rang out in the church.

Without a doubt, grandpa did not hesitated with a humorous response. He replied, "It was some swallowing going on any way." Once again, laughter from the congregation could be heard outside the church building. As the sermon continued, an old lady seated at the back of the church shouted loudly, "What's this in Dumfries Church?" The audience responded once again with laughter that echoed throughout the church.

Just as grandpa was about to conclude his sermon, the youngest of his grandsons entered the church and sat on the wooden bench at the back. Grandpa must have been distracted by his grandson's sudden appearance that he shouted from the top of his voice, "Beauford, you been to the goat?" The benediction was given and everyone left the service consumed with joy and much humor.

Sweet Island Life

CHAPTER 13
The Bad Blow Hole

The story of the Bad Blow Hole has originated over several generations. People who tell the story must have knowledge of the formation of blow holes on the island and the danger it posed for those who were unexperienced swimmers.

Researches of underground caves have documented proof that strong current from the ocean flows directly into blow holes which causes the water level to rise and fall with the tide.

Listen to Sammy Ring's story as he gave his account of a large creature living in the bad blow hole and how the natives were afraid. The school children had gathered in the yard, they formed a semicircle and sat on the rocks just to hear the story of the bad blow hole. Some of them were very young and had limited knowledge of a blow hole.

It was summer, the dew had settled in the valley, and the rays of the sun appeared over the trees in the Mangrove swamp. One of Sammy's favorite horses had died and he didn't want to burn the carcass, neither did he wanted to bury it. He decided to dispose of it by pushing it over the cliff into the bad blow hole.

Splash! Was the sound of the horse as it entered the deep blue water and floated away from the cliff where the men stood watching with anticipation. Several minutes had passed, then suddenly there were movements in the water about one hundred feet from the carcass. A huge two headed creature rose from deep blue waters with opened jaws, yellow eyes, and sharp pointed teeth. It snatched the carcass from the surface and slowly disappeared leaving behind a swirling pool of bloody water.

Sammy Ring was speechless. The men who assisted him ran away as fast as they could leaving behind all that they had brought with them. Everyone who had heard about the encounter at the bad blow hole would not venture near it again.

This story had captured the attention of the students who sat patiently and listened to Sammy Ring's story. Without a doubt, it had prepared them for the descriptive assignment at school and highlighted the risk of swimming in the bad blow hole.

CHAPTER 14
Down Home Connection

The Down Home rhythm of the rake and scrape music is the cultural bed rock of the Bahamas. Those who are accustomed to the rhythm of the music on Cat Island can appreciation the rich heritage of it's people while they dance, prance and twist their bodies to an electrifying experience. So, join in this cultural expression and capture the experience of a new song.

Down Home .... With the Rake & Scrape
Oh! Down Home .... With Flour Cake
Down Home .... With Stew Fish & Jonny Bread
Oh! Down Home .... Guinee Corn Grits & Lard
Down Home .... With Flour Pap
Oh! Down Home .... Lime Tea
Down Home .... With Cornbread
Oh! Down Home .... Quadrille Dance
Down Home .... With Crab & Dough
Oh! Down Home .... With Strong Bark
Down Home .... With Fever Grass
Oh! Down Home .... Fishing on the Rock
Down Home .... Visiting Como Hill
Oh! Down Home .... At the Meeting House
Down Home .... Bay Rum
Oh! Down Home .... Cock Bush
Down Home .... Love Vine

"Island living means having a front row seat of nature's performance."

- A. Merhing -

Sweet Island Life

Island life,

Island days,

Island ways.

Surf, Sand, and Sunny Rays!

Live your life while in Paradise.

There is no choice, you will live a longer life.

- Sonia Chae-Telusca -

Resource Information

The writer's research on the subject of Bush Medicine and general interest, credited those family members, natives and friends who are well acquainted with such practices for more than a generation. There are limited number of books written on the subject but the natives of the island have ensured that the name of each plant species are known to family members.

Of course, the opportunity that I had to collect many species of plants gave me the opportunity to examine and describe the similarity and differences for the readers of this book. Although I have not sample every product, I knew of individuals and family members who spoke positively about the magic of bush medicine.

My personal experiences along with testimonies from others who have lived their entire life on the island have provided credible evidence to support the healing properties of bush medicine. However, modern researches have broaden the scope which can be beneficial for further documented evidence on this vital cultural Bahamian heritage.

The following Resource Information is available:

- A Comprehensive Book on Bahamian Bush Medicine
  Mccormack K, Mair and Wallens

- Bahamian Bush Medicine Garden
  Richard (Blue) Jones

- Bush Medicine of the Bahamas
  Jeffrey Holt mccormack Ph. D

- Bush Medicine in the Bahamas Folk Tradition
  Hanna-Smith M (2005)

- Phil Stubbs, a native of Cat Island

Sweet Island Life

About the Author

Nevelon Theophilus Gaitor was born on the eighth largest island in the Commonwealth of the Bahamas. He is a native of Cat Island but has migrated to the island of New Providence in the late seventies to further his education and chartered a new course in life.

He is a certified-professional high school teacher, a veteran educator and has served in the position as Vice Principal Ministry of Education Science and Technology for many years. He presently serves as the District Education Officer at the Southern Secondary District Office, New Providence, Bahamas. He has successfully completed the Educational Management certification course sponsored by The Department of Education. He is a graduate of The College of the Bahamas, The University of The West Indies Board of Education, and Saint Benedict College & Saint John's University Collegeville, Minnesota, U. S. A.

Mr. Nevelon Gaitor is the author of the book entitled "A Collection of Smart Comments for Report Cards." He resides with his wife Olive and children, Kenya Gaitor-Ferguson, and Kerim Ormond Jason Gaitor at Golden Gates #2, Nassau Bahamas. His spiritual foundation is built on biblical principles and the belief that he can do all things through Christ who strengthens him. He has a passion for education, a vision for the future and a commitment to ensure that the importance of historical cultural values are preserved not only for the people who presently exist but for generations unborn. It is his hope that the manifestation of a rich cultural heritage would come alive on the stage of theatres both locally and internationally.

His hobbies include reading, music, backyard farming and carpentry. He is a native of Cat Island and is proud to be a Bahamian.

The History Of
Cat Island
Bahamas

NEVELON T. GAITOR

Made in United States
North Haven, CT
29 January 2023

31830391R00036